ORANGES

Poems from Maharishi School

Edited by Cliff Yates

Maharishi School Press

First published in 2001
by Maharishi School Press
Maharishi School
Cobbs Brow Lane
Lathom
Ormskirk
Lancs L40 6JJ

All proceeds from this book go to
Maharishi School (New Beacon School
Registered Charity No. 517958)

© Cover illustration by David Williams 2001

ISBN 09541785-0-5

Typeset and printed by Chesil Press

Contents

Maharishi School

Maharishi School is a non-selective, mixed, independent school near Skelmersdale, Lancashire, with 100 children on roll, age 4-16. The school offers Consciousness-Based Education, incorporating the practice of Transcendental Meditation, an easily-learned effortless technique, practised for 15-20 minutes twice daily which settles the mind and body to a unique state of restful alertness, allowing the mind to naturally experience the level of its own full potential, Transcendental Consciousness.

Research verifies that the experience of Transcendental Consciousness is uniquely effective in activating the latent reserves in the brain. With regular practice of the Transcendental Meditation technique, the immense creative intelligence inherent in every individual increasingly expresses itself in thought and action.

Derek Cassells
HEADTEACHER

Foreword

The work that Cliff Yates has done for poetry with children, and for children with poetry, is exceptional and heartening. He is at once expert and inspiring – always proving how necessary it is to recognise that 'creating' is a vital part of 'educating.'

His anthologies perform the same function: they make fun a part of their function, and play a part of their purpose. This selection, like the rest of his work, deserves to be cherished.

Andrew Motion
POET LAUREATE

Introduction

Oranges brings together the award-winning poems and the poems published in the *Times Educational Supplement* Young Poet column, written by Maharishi School pupils during the last seven years. I hadn't realised there were so many poems; due to lack of space I haven't been able to include commendations in W H Smith Young Writers, or our runners-up in the Simon Elvin Young Poet Awards, another 56 poems.

Events such as the *TES* Young Poet and The Simon Elvin awards present brilliant opportunities for young writers, and demonstrate that writing by young people can and should be taken seriously. They also provide pupils with a wider audience for their work, and they give teachers a useful excuse to get pupils to re-draft their poems. Strange as it may sound in this context, I tell pupils that winning awards or getting published is not the most important thing. Writing poems with the intention of winning a competition would, I reckon, be like trying to swim with a weight tied to your ankle. My priorities are to show pupils how to write (using good poems as examples), to give them confidence in their work, and to establish an atmosphere where writing poems is valued for its own sake.

You will find the background to *Oranges* in my handbook *Jumpstart Poetry in the Secondary School*. Teachers will be able to detect the influence of the poems that the pupils have been reading, and the strategies behind them. For example a poem written in a numbered sequence probably indicates that we had been reading '13 Ways of Looking at a Blackbird' by Wallace Stevens. A poem based on a character using a series of images probably originated in the furniture game, where pupils generate metaphors by asking each other (or themselves) questions such as 'if this character were a piece of fruit, what would they be? Having said that, the poems, even within these categories, are varied. I encourage the pupils to surprise me in their writing, and tell them that when they write well they will surprise themselves.

I hope you enjoy *Oranges*. If teachers who read this book go back into their classrooms with a handful of new ideas borrowed from the poems, or if young people read it and decide to have a go at writing for themselves, that will be great.

Cliff Yates
SKELMERSDALE, NOVEMBER 2001

An hour in the life

Swayin' in de breeze
In de palm treeze
With de big fat juicy green
Leevze

Swimmin' in de sea
Is a little fishy
Smilin' up to
Me

At de bar
Is me grandpa
Swiggin'
From a jar

On de sand
Is de rock an' roll band
Playin', playin'
Grand

RUTH HITE

Maybe there's a...

Maybe there's a batskin cloak
All crumpled up in there.
Or maybe there's an elephant skin
Or Grandad's underwear.

There could be Mum's first valentine
Or an adder with a lisp
Or a completely squashed up butterfly
Or a mouldy purple crisp.

Maybe there's a tortoise
Beneath that rusty shell
Or a camel that's not lumpy
Or an old Tibetan bell.

Maybe Mum could tell me
What's in that battered tin.
I wonder if she would mind
If I had just a tiny look in.

KATE LINES

Love Ballad to a Scott Boulder Mountain Bike, 16in Frame in Metallic Grey/Silver £625 ono

Scott, oh Scott, where have you gone
with your chunky, grey
"Psycho" tyres, so precious
to me?

No more Shimano Deore LX
derailleurs, or Mavic M236
rims, Tektro brake levers
simple, easy to hold

I'm not on a diet
but I've lost 27 pounds
approx.

Now you've gone away
I'm lost in a flat land, clean,
without my double-butted chromoly frame,
what can I do?

Swim?

RUTH HITE

A Portrait of Sherlock Holmes

Street lamps glimmer
in the smoky night
of Victorian London.
In a tall, dark house,
a pipe smoulders
on a mantlepiece
and a violin leans against a wall
echoing tunes
played long ago.
A bloodhound
lies by a crackling fire
watching
a fly, landing on
a Venus fly-trap.
Like a fish
swimming into the net.
Or a unsuspecting criminal
falling into the snare
of a master detective.

KATE LINES

The Merchant of Sweat

Lifting weights,
Like a huge
10 mile thick
titanium
wall

A big sweaty chair
A dune-filled desert
A giant foaming
lager

A roast bull
dripping
A robot
in a psycho-type
film
A very solid
oak tree
A sweat merchant
Arnold Schwarzenegger

JAMIE SCOTT

Stork

I am hungry.
Razor-sharp beak
poised
to snatch
a silver-scaled trout
from the murky, shallow water.

I wait patiently
for my dinner.

I look down
at my thin, long legs
like chopsticks
protruding
from a feather bed
and feel

slightly ridiculous.
I hope the trout don't laugh.

THOMAS YATES

The Chompachoo

A lion's mane and a guinea pig's head
An octopus's tail and 25 legs
Butterfly's fingernails and ladybird's knees
A dragon's body and a liking for peas

Eyes like an owl and a Cheshire cat's smile
Hawk's talons and wings like coral
Rabbit's ears and its noise is moo
What could it be but a Chompachoo?

RUTH YATES

Bath Towel

Draped over a radiator,
I'm drying off.

The morning comes and with it –
the odour of my lover.
Squinting as the sun shines
bright through the blinds.

The rain over her is more
like a storm,
but no rainbow appears.

She rubs me over her,
like sandpaper on a table top.

Draped over the radiator
to dry off again.

He walks in unaware
of our love affair.

OLIVER BRIERLEY

The Lesser Spotted Yellow Ankle-Biter

Sitting
pancaked against the ground
waits

like a mine
teeth bared
gurgling

An eye darts
from side to side
nervously

Munch!

MICHAEL TAYLER

Second Class

You are desecrated,
dirtied by strange
curving lines of blue.

Bent over, you are
ignominously thrust into
a confining, dark space.

You are, at present,
experiencing claustrophobia.

There is a slurping
wet sound and
you're immured.

You are taken
to a small, brick
building and your death
certificate is carefully pasted
onto the
top right-hand corner
of your prison.

Then, you are carelessly
pushed into the
gaping,
dark maw
of the post-box.

THOMAS YATES

If Only...

I'm a
discontented cordless Kenwood kettle.

I dream
of greasy crumbs and
4 slice bread slots.
A toaster!
A shiny
green
Morphy Richards toaster, with
Variable Browning Control.

And I'd slouch
with my Frozen Bread Setting
and my Touch-sensitive Reheat Button,
while popping reassuringly...

I never had the intellect.

LUKE YATES

Lament of a Pear

The pear stands there
On the table
Gazing at the apple
Whose delicate rosy blush
Shines seductively...

"You are the queen" he thinks,
"Perched upon the shoulders
Of your fellows, in your woven throne,
Where I am but as unworthy as
An avocado, to be before your grace.

Look down at my rags,
Brown and green with grime.
How can I compare with your
Soft red dress and teal labels?
So I stand here, below your worship

And admire."

MATALIN HATCHARD

Poem Called Owl

Teddy-bear sits patiently,
Left alone in the woods,
Forgotten.
At night
He preens himself
As teddy-bears do.
Stuffing
Falls.

The lighthouse swings its searching
Beam of vision, out
Across the sea of darkness.
Watching and waiting,
Motionless

As every tiny movement –
The waves and ripples in the dark ocean –
Are silently observed.

Then the shrapnel falls:

The tiger pounces,
Claws and teeth gleaming
In the moonlight.
They sink
Into the little parcel of flesh

And the dead mouse rises.

RUTH HITE

A Jet-Lagged Pineapple Outside a Greengrocers

You squat proudly on armoured
powerful haunches, like a
coiled spring. Trapped in a
roofless prison of coloured
cardboard, attempting to
catch up on some much-needed
sleep, you daydream of hot,
wet tropical forests.

Scaly eyelids blink, then open to
stare at the blatantly obtrusive
forest of tanned, hairy
tree trunks which have
sprouted up around you.

Wishing (not unreasonably)
that someone had remembered
to build your cell a roof,
you crouch, muttering angrily,
like an old, crusty hunk of
punk, balding
dough.

THOMAS YATES

Tiger

Kitty cat, Big kitty cat
was once a tiger
now a mat.

Fur and whiskers, tail and paws,
stripes and eyes, nose and claws.

A bullet hits,
blood, crash,
disappears in a flash.

Kitty cat, Big kitty cat
was once a tiger
now a mat.

ARABELLA HIGGINS

The Life of a Piece of Seaweed

I'd like to be some seaweed
and floppily lie on the sands
while the sea laps my head and legs
and dozily licks my hands.

I'd like to be some seaweed
and dream a seaweed dream
I'd have a salt bath every day
and stay immaculately clean.

I'd like to be some seaweed
I'd never have to work
I'd lazily, dozily, floppily, poppily
on the wet sand lurk.

RUTH YATES

Mist

Eyes feel misted up,
shortsighted and wearing
grey glasses.
Silent weird shapes
further away in black
and white.
Fingering groping trees
ask the sky why it has deserted them.

It creeps in at night
when lampposts are steaming
and roads are wet.
The world
stifled.

LUKE YATES

Images of a Pair of Scissors

* Today's weather will be cloudy with sunny patches and
                    occasional thunderstorms in the South
* Builders wearing plastic hats and steel boots
* The tin man is wearing a bow in his hair
* Open - indicating treasure for pirates
* Closed - a carving knife with a very bent handle
* On the smoky road to lung cancer
* A heron, flying, yawns
* Through the shiny sea slid a shark's fin
* Wearing orange knickers, these legs have no shoes
* One of three important things in a child's game
* Celebration, inauguration, invitation and destruction

KATE LINES

6 Ways of Looking at a Telephone

1.
Take your ready-mixed telephone and chop roughly.
Stir-fry for 10-12 minutes, stirring frequently in a deep pan,
adding water when required.
Toss with freshly-cut answer-phone messages to taste.

2.
The telephone rang five times.
The man concealed a small package
in the lining of his overcoat,
pulled his brim over his eyes
and strode out.

3.
The small child is in four minds;
his mother is in the bath, his father is out.
The telephone is ringing, the doorbell rings.
Should he answer the telephone? The door?
Neither? Both?

4.
He has set the burglar alarm.
He has locked the door.
He has taken off his clothes.
The telephone rings.

5.
How do I stand people prodding my exclusive
Big Button Keypad,
yelling into my Hearing-aid Compatible Receiver,
as if someone is going to answer them?
FORGET my PABX Alternative,
AND my 13 Direct Messages,
AND my New LCD Display. Leave me alone!

6.
He was silhouetted in the sunset.
I gave a faint cry and swooned,
but he caught me in his arms.
The telephone rang.

LUKE YATES

7 Adventures of a Budgie

1.
The budgie prances moodily around the cage.
My little sister, standing on the table, imitates him.
Someone peers through the window and hurries away.

2.
A short, fat man tries on his new bathing costume.
A loud raspberry sounds behind him. He spins round.
The budgie smirks to itself in the corner of its cage.

3.
Auntie May's budgie has escaped.
We search all the neighbouring gardens.
The budgie, perched on a roof tile, watches with interest.

4.
It is the morning of the first of April.
The children are unusually quiet.
On the dining room table, under a tea cosy,
the budgie waits expectantly
in the company of a hamster in the egg cup.

5.
There is a loud splashing coming from the bathroom.
A little child creeps forward.
Is it a ghost?
The budgie bathes happily in bath foam.

6.
A cat is chasing our budgie.
Dad throws a shoe.
The cat dashes under the fence
to glower at the gloating budgie.

7.
Granny is knitting.
On the floor beside her is a lot of pink wool,
a half knitted sock
and a tangled-up budgie.

RUTH YATES

Bluebottles

The small black spudges on the wall
A graveyard
For bluebottles.

The buzz of the radio
Or is it a bluebottle?

In the privacy of the bathroom
No one can see you
Except maybe the bluebottle on the lampshade.

Black car, mourning?
Not for the bluebottle squashed on
The Sunday Times.

PENNY BUSWELL

The Porpoise of Life

The porpoise of life
according
to the law of porpoises
is
   eating
        sleeping
   and looking like
a disused vacuum cleaner
dragged unwillingly
   from
       the cupboard
          under the stairs.

RUTH YATES

His/Her

His

Guilt was sitting by a pond
throwing stones into dark water.
Conscience sat beside her
and chewed its nails.

Her

Hate came in.
She gave me some scissors.
We started a fire
and cut the heads off your photos.

Jealousy followed some way behind.
Painting the room a livid green.
We tore your clothes
and threw them out onto the street.

Malice is the fourth sister.
Stepping from the shadows in the corner of the room.
Her double-edged dagger
glinting silver in the light.

Now they are gone
and Sorrow emerges from behind the door.

CATHERINE PAINTER–CHAPMAN

James Bond

The moveable trolley rockets
Down the privy
Looking for
A restored Aston Martin
Which was looking for
An old stately home.

1964 Fantasy Novel.
Live for the moment;
The glamour, the fame
The thrill
Of when the dining
Room table with 50
seated guests
Galahants into
The kitchen.

WILLIAM KERLEY

Dehydrated in the English Room

Parched with thirst
We loll on our desks
Trying to drink
Bottles of Quink.

We cannot pay attention to the English teacher;
Too busy licking lips,
Feeling sick,
Stomachs contracting.

The girls are licking the condensation off the windows
But there isn't much left; the first years have already been at it.
Someone has a chemical from the lab
And it looks like water . . .

Children wasted on the floor, some sucking rubbers cross-eyed,
Cheeks sucked in like goldfish.
Ink bottles empty, children wither in their seats
And the English teacher still hasn't noticed.

LUKE YATES

A Shrill Whistle of Diesel

The umbilical cord is broken
I am separated from the petrol station
for a few pounds,
I rush down the steep oily black stairs
Instinct tells me about my duty
My turn near the friction-heated brake comes,
Then down and up in a long slide
The roar of the double-impact turbo engine silences all,
Through the car's highway
Into the rotating fins
Past the volcano
I vibrate in a long tube
bouncing back and forth
Hesitating whether to go out or to stay in,
Taking a spoonful of bravery
I leap out of the exhaust pipe
Drinking oxygen in gulps
Free from materialism.

EMMANUEL DOIT

Donkey

As you shamble through
    the mud, it sounds
as if you have
    clotted cream between
the weathered cracks of
    your horny hooves.

You snorfle your
    ridiculous nose into
my pockets, as if
    you think you will find
thistles growing between
    the bus tickets,
old coins
    and sweet wrappers.

Try something more
    interesting, or exciting.
Tangle that idea into
    your matted mane and
fuzzy,
      dusty head.

RUTH YATES

An Invasion

Warning

They have landed.
The disembodied thumbs with legs
Are coming.

We inhale them.
They fill our clothes, pillows, mattresses and carpets,
Stinking and itching.

Less than half a millimeter
Of palm tree and sausage
Feeding on dead skin.

Dermatophagoide,
Dust Mite.

BEN CROSS

The Dwarf and the Horse with the Slippery Back

He can just about reach
the stirrups. Bracing himself,
he clings onto them,
walking his feet up the horse's straight leg
until he is upside
down. He slings his short legs
over the horse's
stiff neck and
gripping the long hair, propels
his small body onto the horse's back.
He begins to rock, back
and forth. As he gets higher,
he gets more unsteady.
Suddenly
he is vaulted head
over heels
to the ground.
He will try again soon.

LUKE YATES

How to be a Cat's Eye on the A46

1.
If by rare coincidence,
an idiotic pheasant
should flounder your way
feel free to pluck out
its tailfeathers.

2.
Having a hoard of feathers
is useful. One can
harass cyclists
by entangling such
items into the spokes
of bicycles.

3.
On a dark night,
jump about,
turn upside down
and thoroughly confuse
all drivers.

4.
Keep to the road
and above all,
avoid magpies.

RUTH YATES

Storm on the Motorway

Thousands of rice grains
battle with
Albinoni's adagio
on Classic FM,

Blotted circles
of rain,
Creatures
from microscopes.

Vicky fights a
free-with-chips-and-beans
pink wire
power ranger.

Spiny black
cotton wool trees
sit 2D on
a black and blue landscape.

Paramedics take
the people who couldn't
see through the rain.
Others slow and watch

The traffic cones in the
ditch, scattered
white teeth still
gleaming.

PENNY BUSWELL

The Monster Under My Bed

No one knows about
The monster under my bed.
He's lived there for ten thousand years
Eating my dreams and drinking
My thoughts.
With his black eyes and purple
Hair,
His body the colour of sleep.

AIDAN MOUSLEY

You Could Try Retrieving Your Ball From Our Garden Without Asking But...

The gate's covered
by several highly trained marksmen. One is hiding
in the water-butt. The others
could be anywhere.

There are landmines
on most of the paving stones
and the others are patrolled from 100m up
by rare birds; pitt-bull eagles
you can't miss them
they're the ones with the spiked collars
and tattoos.

You could try the fence
and if you do, just mind the
numerous high-voltage electric wires
and be careful not to snag your jumper
on the dozens of six-inch razor-sharp flick-knives
that are cunningly concealed
within the woodwork.

Once in the garden,
don't feed the rhinos
be sure to dodge all the
six-foot invisible computer-guided explosive-tipped poison darts
that you may encounter
and then start to find your ball.

LUKE YATES

Toad

I grithe through pondwater,
my amphibian crawl
playing on people's feelings;
people who dislike me.

I have no warts.
What you see
is the overflow of my feelings,
popping through my skin.

Have empathy for my
rough body, grobbly feet.

My eyes are friendly; cold like trees,
as I crawl to the pond's edge,
my feet at cross-purposes
to plosh
with a blink
into the stringy water.

RUTH YATES

At Night They Canter

Where the orange-eyed ghoul
of a coat-peg grimaces horrifically
where bare feet are pricked
by the carpet nails
on shadowy stairs.

Light from the torch
spreads in an arc
casting deep gloom
into uninhabited corners, illuminating
three ducks on the wall, wings
beating in perfect time
to the clock's mantis tick.

They are everywhere
you can imagine. Too numerous
to count. Too meaningful, too
unbearingly rhythmic. And then
they begin to get louder. It's almost imperceptible
at first. It gets clearer
louder
until all other sounds
fade away
and it's only the sound of the horse's hooves coming
nearer
and nearer

Silhouettes of plants
on the window sill
growing like beans you can almost hear them moving

LUKE YATES

6 Ways of Looking at a Sofa

1. The flowery cushions
   fiendishly hide under them
   the remote for the T.V.

2. The never-ending sofa sale – 957.653% off

3. They say that he had a heart
   of leather.

4. The sofas came in two by two
   Hurrah, Hurrah…

5. The sofas are closing in
   from all sides
   each one carrying
   a 10mm automatic shotgun
   on each arm.
   They have merciless looks about them.

6. The sofa cannot be trusted.
   It is left alone
   in the lounge with the T.V.
   the stereo
   the 17th century grandfather clock
   and the 3 by 4ft Picasso.
   The sofa curses to itself that
   it is too big
   to fit through the window.

JAMES CHALMERS

Lumb Bank

The windows dense with breath
and cobwebs, to one side
I can see the purply mountain,
a hump of clayish earth, pumping,
spiked with a purple soft mass
of trees, and I feel like that mound
of pulse, quiet on the sun-sharped
day, throbbing like the cat on the lawn,
black and white tufted smooth-spiralled
curling of himself, moving backwards.

RUTH YATES

I Think my Brain is Coming out of my Ears

Found a pink wet thing
like a prawn on my pillow this morning
felt it, smelt it, looked at it under the microscope
and I could see memories, rumours and dreams
scrawled in my handwriting over the surface.
I keep my bit of brain in a jar, feed it marmalade, call it Fred.
Frightening to think what might be missing –
unexplained chunks of life.
(I can't find the remote). Tonight
I sleep, orifices stuffed
and my ears glued to the sides of my head.

LUKE YATES

Melting Butter Over the Toaster

Harry waking me up licking me on the face,
The phone ringing late at night with
John Fuller on the other end,
Being caught reading Harry Potter
Under the cover with my torch,
Mum and Dad honking in the car
Telling me I'm going to be late for school,
My curtains being too thin to stop the summer light,
The hair-dryer stopping after five minutes,
My bin overflowing,
Going for a walk with my dad along the canal,
Not making my bed,
Being able not to miss anything.

JOSIE WILLIAMS

Waiting was Invented in Hell
(Hope and Trust)

Waiting was invented in hell
as your life tick tocks
before eyes that wait.
Troubled thoughts are put to rest
with a dark mask
and metallic blades,
sharp flesh piercing contraptions
find you,
haunt you in your nightmares.
The little green man watches over,
he has your life in his hands.
On this cold unforgiving bed
with monsters of machines
strapped onto you,
miracles are in the making.

DALE SULLIVAN

Who Ate the Mince Pie?

1.
Under your steamy, cavern-like duvet
Cautiously toe the crackly lumps.

2.
Give Fred, the pink-eyed monkey a poke.
Let him know what's going on.

3.
Tear through the familiar wrapping paper
A.S.A.P.

4. Admire plastic twiglet soldiers
As they stand to attention.

5.
Try out new felt tip (labelled Partners).
Happy red faces smile back from the bedroom wall.

6.
Experiment with morphing techniques
Spin round three times, you're:
a tiger
Superman
Buzz Light Year.

7.
Can't help but wonder whether it really was Father Christmas
Who ate the mince pie?

BONNIE MERCER

Terrosit (Edit 3)

Trust,
Terrosit group,
Began
(estimate) 1892.

Due to a 0% activity rating
we suspect rival
terrosit hope was born.

Little is known of
hope.

But we suspect (Edit)
    we know

they are most
active when
trust
      has
an activity rating
of below 10%.

WILLIAM KERLEY

Dandelion Leaves Taste Like Apple Crumble

The dog runs round the old-fashioned pump
practising squirrels.
I stand in the middle
next to a stone trough full of water,
listening to my brothers tell me about dandelion leaves.

The water ripples because of woodpigeons.
I want what they say to be true
that would explain why guinea-pigs
like them so much, and I love apple crumble,
but I am dubious.

Birds shift in the weeping ash
because the dog is trying to climb up
and he is so long.

RUTH YATES

Dusty Eyes

Dusty eyes, white face, rough hairy hands,
long yellow nails
his sheriff's star glimmers in the musty light
and his gun is by his hand waiting for an intruder.

The wood on the floor creaks and the sofa springs
and all, nearly collapses under my weight. The dust
rises and blows out the open window which claps
open and shut. The man keeps on staring forward
not even glancing at me.

I can't think of any conversation while twiddling
my thumbs. The vases are cracked, the wallpaper is
falling off and this whole place looks like it's gonna
collapse.

I decide to walk away back out the old
rickety swinging door. Then all of a sudden I feel
a hand on my shoulder. He turns me round, looks
me in the eye and croaks 'Where do…you…
think you…are going, hmm?'

JAMES BURDETT

By Patrick Darren Connely

Today's homework: write your life story.
Well I was born in Langdon, Essex. July 13th, almost fourteen
                                          years ago.
My name is Patrick, although my Dad preferred Darren. That's
                                          about it.
The detention room is like a greenhouse. No windows open,
                                          just glass
letting the June afternoon heat toast us.

VICKY HOZAIFEH

Weed Wants to Travel
(for Bill and Ben)

On a normal day
you'd see my stalk quiver
towards the moss-free flowerpots
which I live behind.
But underneath there's the legful haze
of my crazy roots encountering
worms. The furious tingle
of spread-eagling round bricks
and buried stones, oval and sea-formed
in perfection – my treasure.
My ambition? To travel.
I want to laugh
my whispery name
down your drainpipe,
to echo and boom when you
turn on your taps.
To slowly drive my legs
through rich earth,
letting a hunch of gathered snails
clatter from my leaves.

RUTH YATES

Tom Bennett's Gold Watch

He's sitting in his comfy chair,
Shouting orders at unsuspecting
Young cargo workers.

He hides me in his double bunk
Behind the freezer with the cans of tinned beans.

Me, 7yrs old,
Listening to his great 'boogie woogie' CD
At 6 in the morning,

His old teddy duck
Sitting faithfully on his lorry mantle-piece,
Waiting to protect him,

Plastic packets of ham and tuna sandwiches
Lying with the crumbs of '86,
in the industrial sized bin up front,

The thunderous engine telling me to strap in
And start eating my plain crackers,
Watching the world go by,
Playing with his shiny gold watch.

PIETER KOEHORST

Acknowledgements

Copyright is owned by the authors of these poems except for: 'If Only...' by Luke Yates, 'Lament of a Pear' by Matalin Hatchard, 'Poem Called Owl' by Ruth Hite and 'Second Class' by Thomas Yates which were published in *Wondercrump Poetry - Poems from the Roald Dahl Foundation Third Poetry Competition* (Red Fox, 1996), where copyright is owned by Random House Children's Books; for 'Images of a Pair of Scissors' by Kate Lines, '6 Ways of Looking at a Telephone' by Luke Yates, and '7 Adventures of a Budgie' by Ruth Yates, which were published in *Inky Foot – Award-Winning Entries from the 1997 W H Smith Young Writers Competition* (Macmillan Children's Books, 1998), where copyright is owned by W H Smith Limited; 'Dehydrated in the English Room' by Luke Yates, 'Donkey' by Ruth Yates and 'An Invasion' by Ben Cross, which were published in *Inky Foot – Award-Winning Entries from the 1998 W H Smith Young Writers' Competition* (Macmillan Children's Books, 1999), where copyright is owned by W H Smith Limited. These poems are printed here with kind permission.

Thanks are also due to the editors of the following publications in which some of these poems appeared: *Hypothesis: Poems by the Simon Elvin Young Poets of 1999*, (The Poetry Society 1999), *Poems on the Underground, The Small Plastic Things in Life: Poems by the Simon Elvin Young Poets of 1998*, (The Poetry Society 1998), *The Rialto, Times Educational Supplement. The TES Book of Young Poets* (Times Educational Supplements Ltd, 1999). We would also like to thank the organisers and sponsors of the competitions in which some of these poems were successful.

Ruth Hite, 13, 'An Hour in the Life,' Kate Lines, 11, 'Maybe There's A...', joint winners, Puffin Poetry Competition, 1994.

Ruth Hite, 14, 'Love Ballad to a Scott Boulder Mountain Bike, 16in Frame in Metallic Grey/Silver £625 ONO,' *Times Educational Supplement* Young Poet, May 12th 1995.

Kate Lines, 12, 'A Portrait of Sherlock Holmes,' *Times Educational Supplement* Young Poet, September 22nd 1995.

Jamie Scott, 12, The Merchant of Sweat' *Times Educational Supplement* Young Poet, October 20th 1995.

Thomas Yates, 14, 'Stork,' *Times Educational Supplement* Young Poet, November 10th 1995.

Ruth Yates, 9, 'The Chompachoo', *Times Educational Supplement* Young Poet, November 17th 1995.

Oliver Brierley, 14, 'Bath Towel', *Times Educational Supplement* Young Poet, January 26th 1996,

Michael Tayler, 13, 'The Lesser Spotted Yellow Ankle-Biter' *Times Educational Supplement* Young Poet, February 9th 1996. Thomas Yates, 15, 'Second Class,' BBC Radio 4 Young Poetry Competition commendation, 1996.

Luke Yates, 11, 'If Only...,' winner; Matalin Hatchard, 14, 'Lament of a Pear,' Ruth Hite, 15, 'Poem Called Owl' and Thomas Yates, 15, 'Second Class,' runners-up, in Roald Dahl Foundation Poetry Competition, 1996 also Maharishi School winners of 'Wondercrump' School Award.

Thomas Yates, 15, 'A Jet-Lagged Pineapple Outside a Greengrocers', TES Young Poet, June 7th 1996. Arabella Higgins, 12, 'Tiger,' runner-up, BBC Blue Peter/World Wildlife Fund National Poetry Day competiton, October 1996.

Ruth Yates, 10, 'The Life of a Piece of Seaweed' *Times Educational Supplement* Young Poet, November 22nd 1996.

Luke Yates, 13, 'Mist.' *Times Educational Supplement* Young Poet, June 13th 1997.

Kate Lines, 14, 'Images of a Pair of Scissors" Luke Yates, 13, '6 Ways of Looking at a Telephone,' Ruth Yates, 11, '7 Adventures of a Budgie' winners, and Penny Buswell, 14, 'Bluebottles,' runner-up, WH Smith Young Writers *Inky Foot* Competition, 1997.

Ruth Yates, 11, 'The Porpoise of Life' *Times Educational Supplement* Young Poet, September 19th 1997, also published in *The TES Book of Young Poets* (Times Educational Supplements Ltd, 1999), and in 'Little School of Calm,' The Times (Saturday magazine) September 5th 1998,

Catherine Painter-Chapman, 13, 'His and Her,' *Times Educational Supplement* Young Poet, November 7th 1997, also in *The TES Book of Young Poets*.

William Kerley, 13, 'James Bond,' *Times Educational Supplement* Young Poet, May 22 1998, also in *The TES Book of Young Poets*.

Emmanuel Doit, 13, 'The Shrill Whistle of Diesel,' *Times Educational Supplement* Young Poet, June 12th 1998.

Luke Yates, 14, 'Dehydrated in the English Room,' Ruth Yates, 12, 'Donkey,' winners, Ben Cross, 15, 'An Invasion,' runner-up, W H Smith Young Writers *Inky Foot* Competition, 1998.

Luke Yates, 14, 'The Dwarf And The Horse With The Slippery Back,' Ruth Yates, 12, 'How to be a Cat's Eye on the A46,' Penny Buswell, 15, 'Storm on the Motorway,' winners, Simon Elvin Young Poet Awards, 1998 organised by the Poetry Society; winners' poems published in *The Small Plastic Things in Life*, (Poetry Society, 1999).

Luke Yates, 14, 'Dehydrated in the English Room,' *Times Educational Supplement* Young Poet October 2nd 1998.

Aidan Mousley, 13, 'The Monster Under My Bed,' *Times Educational Supplement* Young Poet, February 5th 1999.

Luke Yates, 15, 'You Could Try Retrieving Your Ball From Our Garden Without Asking But…,' Ruth Yates, 13, 'Toad,' winners, Simon Elvin Young Poet Awards 1999 organised by the Poetry Society; winners' poems published in *Hypothesis: Poems by the Simon Elvin Young Poets of 1999*, (The Poetry Society 1999).

Luke Yates, 15, 'At Night They Canter,' joint second prize, Young Persons' Poetry Competition, *The Rialto*, April 2000.

James Chalmers, 12, '6 Ways of Looking at a Sofa,' *Times Educational Supplement* Young Poet, June 16th 2000.

Ruth Yates, 14, 'Lumb Bank,' *Times Educational Supplement* Young Poet, June 30th 2000.

Luke Yates, 16, 'I think my brain is coming out of my ears,' winner of the Young Poets on the Underground competition, August 2000; poem displayed on London Underground and to be published in the tenth edition of *Poems on the Underground* (Cassell).

Josie Williams, 13, 'Melting Butter Over the Toaster', *Times Educational Supplement* Young Poet, November 10th 2000.

Dale Sullivan, 15, 'Waiting Was Invented in Hell: Hope and Trust,' *Times Educational Supplement* Young Poet, March 2nd 2001. Bonnie Mercer, 15, 'Who Ate the Mince Pie?' winner, William Kerley, 16, 'Terrosit (Edit 3),' Ruth Yates, 15, 'Dandelion Leaves Taste Like Apple Crumble,' runners-up, 'Childline' competition, April 2001.

James Burdett, 14, 'Dusty Eyes,' *Times Educational Supplement* Young Poet, July 6th 2001. Vicky Hozaifeh, 12, 'By Patrick Darren Connely,' Pieter Koehorst, 14, 'Tom Bennett's Gold Watch,' Ruth Yates, 15, 'Weed Wants to Travel,' winners, Simon Elvin Young Poet Awards, 2001.

Pieter Koehorst, 14, 'Tom Bennett's Gold Watch,' *Times Educational Supplement* Young Poet, 26th October 2001